ART 123

Stefano Zuffi

Abrams Books for Young Readers
New York

1

woman gazing into the sun.
Is it setting
or has the day just begun?

Caspar David Friedrich
Woman before the Setting Sun, c. 1818

Oil on canvas, 22,5 x 30 cm
Museum Folkwang, Essen

2

Good afternoon, my king, my queen.
Are you enjoying this winter scene?

Henry Moore
King and Queen, 1952-53

Bronze, 170 x 150 x 95 cm
Middelheim Museum, Antwerp

3

men in hats gather for a game.
One might be cheating – who is to blame?

Caravaggio
The Cardsharps, 1594

Oil on canvas, 94.2 x 130.9 cm
Kimbell Art Museum, Fort Worth

4

In the dark and lonely night,
4 people stay together in the light.

Edward Hopper
Nighthawks, 1942

Oil on canvas, 84.1 x 152.4 cm
The Art Institute of Chicago

**happy dancing girls.
See how their circle twirls and twirls!**

Henri Matisse
Dance, 1909-10

Oil on canvas, 260 x 391 cm
The State Hermitage Museum, St. Petersburg

6

*lazy kittens on the floor.
Some stretch and curl,
others sleep some more.*

Thomas Gainsborough
Six Studies of a Cat, 1765-70

Black and white crayon on coloured paper, 33.2 x 45.9 cm
Rijksmuseum, Amsterdam

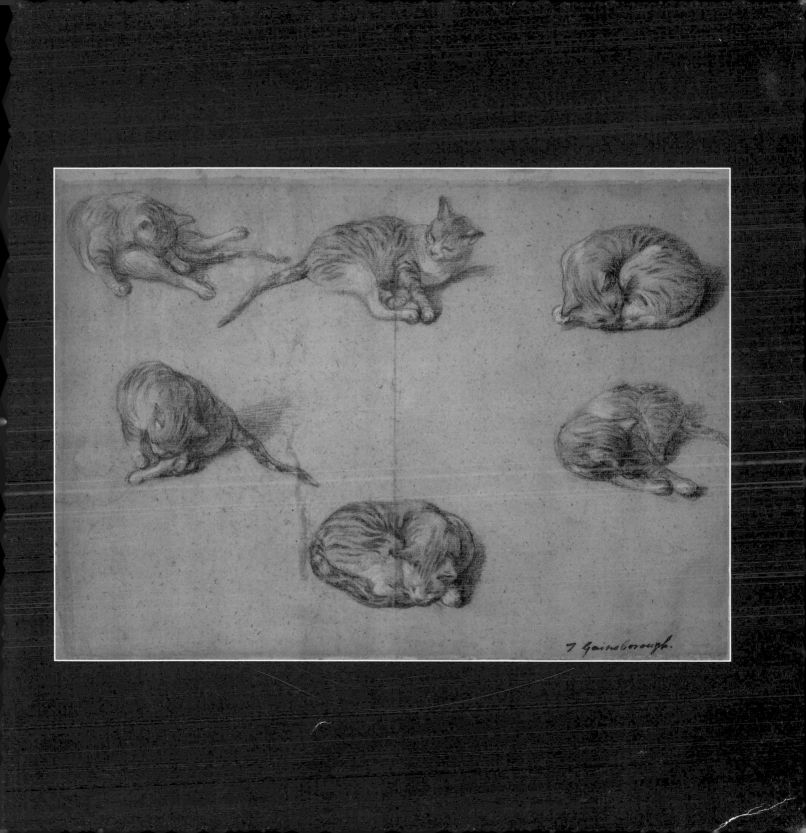

rays of sun illuminate the skies.
Let the day begin – open up your eyes!

Roy Lichtenstein
Sunrise, 1965

Oil on canvas, 91.4 x 172.7 cm
Private collection

8

little boats,
4 on the beach and 4 on the sea.
And is that a treasure chest I see?

Vincent Van Gogh
Fishing Boats on the Beach at Les Saintes-Maries-de-la-Mer, 1888

Oil on canvas, 65 x 81.5 cm
Van Gogh Museum, Amsterdam

9

In a forest full of lovely flowers,
9 people dance away the hours.

Sandro Botticelli
Spring (Primavera), c. 1482

Tempera on panel, 203 x 314 cm
Galleria degli Uffizi, Florence

10

Squares, triangles, rectangles too.
I see 10 in all,
how about you?

Piet Mondrian
Tableau No. IV; Lozenge Composition with Red, Gray, Blue, Yellow, and Black, c. 1924/1925

Oil on canvas, 142.8 x 142.3 cm
National Gallery of Art, Washington D.C.

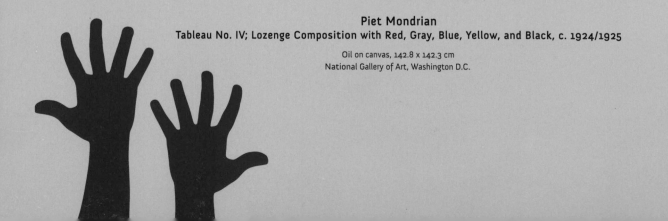

11

A big burning sun shines overhead.
It lights up a leopard, a person,
and 11 flowers, some red.

Henri J.F. Rousseau (Le Douanier)
Virgin Forest with Setting Sun, 1910

Oil on canvas, 114 x 162.5 cm
Kunstmuseum Basel

12

Welcome to this wonderful feast.
We have food and wine
for 12 guests at least!

Pierre-Auguste Renoir
The Luncheon of the Boating Party, 1881

Oil on canvas, 129.5 x 172.7 cm
The Phillips Collection, Washington D.C.

So many

men in hats falling from the sky!
Too many to count,
or will you want to try?

René Magritte
Golconda, 1953

Oil on canvas, 80.7 x 100.6 cm
The Menil Collection, Houston

Design
quod. voor de vorm.

Printed and bound
in Belgium by Proost, Turnhout

Cataloging-in-Publication Data has been applied for and may be obtained from the Library of Congress.
ISBN: 978-1-4197-0100-9

10 9 8 7 6 5 4 3 2 1

Abrams Books for Young Readers are available at special discounts when purchased in quantity for premiums and promotions as well as fundraising or educational use. Special editions can also be created to specification. For details, contact special-sales@abramsbooks.com or the address below.

ABRAMS
THE ART OF BOOKS SINCE 1949

115 West 18th Street
New York, NY 10011
www.abramsbooks.com